Castles and Mansions

Alan James

Lerner Publications Company
Minneapolis

All words printed in **bold** are explained
in the glossary on page 30.

*The author wishes to dedicate this book
to Eric Claussen.*

Cover illustration *Leeds Castle, in Kent, England, was
built as a fortified manor house, and later became a
royal palace.*

First published in the U.S. in 1989 by Lerner Publications
Company.

Library of Congress Cataloging-in-Publication Data

James, Alan, 1943-
    Castles and mansions.

    Bibliography: p.
    Includes index.
    Summary: Discusses castles, manor houses, mansions,
and other large fortified dwellings throughout history.
    1. Castles—Juvenile literature. 2. Mansions—
Juvenile literature. 3. Vernacular architecture—
Juvenile literature. [1. Castles. 2. Mansions.
3. Dwellings] I. Title.
NA7710.J36   1989   728.8   88-23106
ISBN 0-8225-2128-8 (lib.bdg.)

Printed in Italy by G. Canale and C.S.p.A., Turin
Bound in the United States of America

1 2 3 4 5 6 7 8 9 10 98 97 96 95 94 93 92 91 90 89

Contents

Fortified buildings

Throughout history, people of all **civilizations** have needed homes where they could protect themselves against their enemies. Strong defenses, or **fortifications**, were built to provide protection against attack.

A castle was a home built by a king or a nobleman who had conquered a new land and needed to prevent his enemies from winning it back. A castle was a fortress, built in such a way as to provide protection for the owner's family and possessions.

The word "castle" usually refers to the fortifications built after the **Normans** invaded Britain in 1066, but many fortifications were built all over the world before this date. The first forts to be built were hill forts. These were built in high places so that the defenders could see enemies at a distance. It is still possible to see the remains of Maiden Castle in Dorset, England, a huge hill fort built in the Iron Age (anywhere from 2,500 to 4,000 years ago).

The Romans learned a great deal by examining the remains of their enemies' old fortifications, and they developed their own building skills when they took over Europe. The Romans built forts throughout their vast empire to protect their troops. Early forts were built of wood, but these were later replaced by forts built of stone. Large Roman forts were made up of many buildings

Right In Dorset, Britain, the remains of Maiden Castle—a huge hill fort built in the late Iron Age—still stand. The large ditches that surround the area provided defense against attack.

4

surrounded by thick walls, gates, and **turrets**.

Inside, a fort could hold hundreds of soldiers. A Roman fort included a chapel where the **regimental standard** was kept, a bakehouse, a bath house, and large barracks where soldiers slept. A village of **civilians** often grew up outside a fort.

The name given to a Roman fort was *castrum*, meaning "fortified place," and it is from this term that we get our word "castle." However, these forts were not strictly castles. A castle was the private fortress of a ruler which served as his or her home and the base from where he or she defended the land.

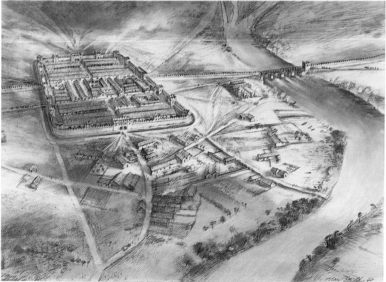

Above The Great Wall of China is a fortification built several thousand years ago. When completed, it stretched some 4,000 miles (6,436 km) in length.

Left The Romans built many forts similar to that shown for their soldiers throughout Europe.

Wooden castles

The earliest true castles were called **motte and bailey** castles and were built in Britain after the Norman Conquest in the eleventh century. William the Conqueror and his **barons** from France knew a great deal about the military use of castles because they had used them to defeat enemies in their own country.

Early castles consisted of a small fort (or keep) built on a small hill with a flat top, called a motte. The keep was surrounded by a fence or **palisade** made up of sharp wooden stakes. At the foot of the motte was a circular courtyard, called the bailey, with a few buildings inside. The bailey of a larger castle contained a kitchen, a chapel, an **armory**, stables, sheds, a bakehouse, and a brewery for making ale. A ditch surrounded the outside of the bailey fence, which had a built-in **drawbridge** that could be raised or lowered over the ditch.

A motte and bailey castle

Keep

Motte

Bailey

Palisade

Drawbridge

The keep and the buildings in the bailey were all built of wood or **wattle and daub.** The keep was built of strong timber, several stories high. The keep basement was usually kept as a storeroom. Above this, reached by a flight of stairs, was the hall or living room. On the next floor, in the area under the roof was the **solar,** or private sitting room and sleep chamber. The keep on top of the motte was the safest place to be if enemy soldiers broke into the bailey.

Above Many wooden castles were built in Normandy in France. This detail from the Bayeux Tapestry shows an attack on a motte and bailey castle at Dinan.

Although large numbers of these castles were built, many of them were replaced by stone towers or walls in later years. Stone walls provided greater protection against enemies than wooden castles.

7

Stone castles

Wooden castles were easily destroyed by fire, so by the middle of the twelfth century many wooden castles began to be replaced by strong stone castles. In places where stone was readily available, it was used instead of wood; otherwise, stone was used to strengthen the walls of existing wooden castles.

A stone wall, called a **curtain wall**, was built around a bailey. This wall had **battlements**—regular gaps along the tops of the walls. Inside the castle wall, a stone keep was built. It was so heavy that it was usually built on flat, solid ground rather than on a motte, which would have been unable to support it.

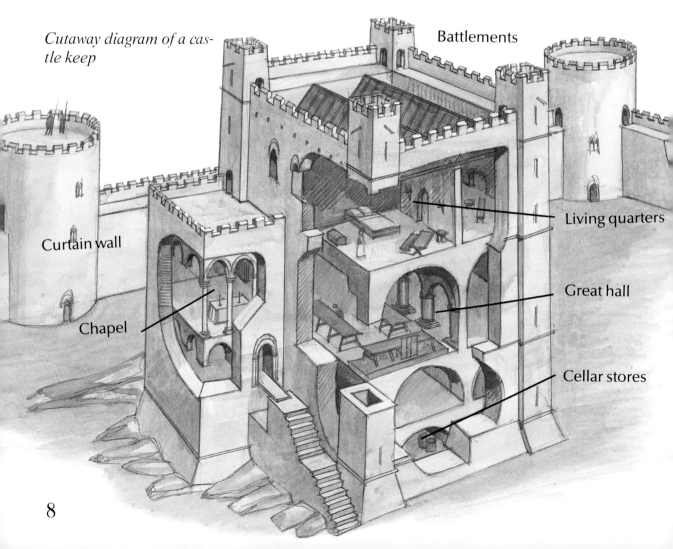

Cutaway diagram of a castle keep

Battlements

Living quarters

Curtain wall

Great hall

Chapel

Cellar stores

8

Right At Restmorel Castle in Britain, a shell keep replaced the wooden palisade at the top of the motte. Inside the shell are stone buildings.

The castle keep held the personal possessions and sleeping quarters of the castle's owners. Above the basement storeroom, the first floor of the keep was occupied by the great hall, where the lord and lady received visitors and held banquets. In early castles, the family would sleep in an alcove in the thick walls, but later the bedroom was usually the room above the hall. Most castles had a private chapel for the family, and a **privy**, but no kitchen because the cooking usually took place in a building in the bailey.

Despite the solid appearance of the large, square, stone keeps, they had their weaknesses and were gradually replaced by **shell keeps**. Some of the earliest stone castles used this design. A shell keep was a strong circular wall often built around the motte of an old wooden castle. The wooden castles were destroyed to make way for buildings of stone. Sometimes these keeps had round rather than square walls. This was because the corners of square keeps were easier for enemies to chisel or break. By the thirteenth century, the circular wall and round tower had become common all over Europe.

The changing design of castles was influenced by the methods of attack and defense in warfare.

Attack

Although a castle was a home, nobody living inside could forget that it was also a fortress, designed to keep an enemy out. An attacking army was faced with a very difficult task when trying to get inside a castle.

The attackers relied on speed, surprise, and skill to invade a castle. One method was to try to stop food

Above *The ruins of Château Gaillard, a strong fortress in France*

and supplies from entering a castle. When the people inside ran out of stores, they were forced to come out. Sometimes the enemy was able to trick someone inside a castle into opening a gate or lowering the drawbridge.

In the days before guns and explosives, attackers would try to scale castle walls or knock them down. There were many weapons that were used to damage a castle. Attackers might try to force their way in using a battering ram. This device was a strong tree trunk with an iron tip. Teams of men rammed the tip against the castle gate or walls.

Other machines, such as the catapult, used the power of twisted ropes to throw heavy stones at the castle. A trebuchet, or "bouncer," was a huge catapult used to hurl heavy rocks or stones at castle walls or to throw missiles over them into the bailey.

Attackers might also use tall ladders to try to climb over the castle walls. Great wooden siege towers were built and propped up against the walls. These protected the attackers from the fire of arrows from overhead.

Siege tower

Trebuchet

Battering-ram

Attacking a castle

Sometimes miners, called "sappers," tunneled under the corners of a castle. They then propped up the tunnel roof with wooden supports and set fire to it. As the wood burned, the tunnel and part of the wall fell in. This method was used as part of the attack on Château Gaillard in France, one of the most difficult castles to enter in the whole of Europe.

Defense

The **siege** of a castle could last for several weeks or months. No food could reach the castle during this time. The people in a castle tried to keep huge stores of supplies, enough to last them as long as a year.

Many castles were well fortified against attack. By the fourteenth century, most castles had a drawbridge, which could be lifted in times of attack, over a ditch or moat. The entrance to the castle was blocked by a huge gate covered with sheet iron, called a **portcullis.**

The portcullis was controlled from the **gatehouse.** The gatehouse contained winding devices to raise and lower the drawbridge and portcullis. Some castles had several portcullises at the main gate, and enemies could become trapped between them. Often there was a **murder-hole** in the ceiling above the passageway where missiles could be dropped on the heads of the attackers.

Defenders would fight from the safety of the castle towers. They fired arrows from the top of the battlement walls, or from the arrow slits at various levels in the castle walls. From this height, defenders could drop missiles on the enemy below. Wooden hoards (shelters which hung out over the walls) with slatted floors were attached to the top of the castle walls for this purpose. Sometimes the defenders poured boiling liquid, or a burning substance called "Greek fire," on the enemy soldiers below.

Left The gatehouse of Harlech Castle, Wales, was strong enough to hold out when the rest of the castle had been overrun by the enemy.

Greek Fire

Portcullis

Hoards

Moat

While defenders pour
burning liquids from above,
attackers float bales of straw
in an attempt to cross the
moat. In this drawing, the
drawbridge has been
eliminated to show the
portcullis.

If the defenders had to surrender,
usually it was because they lacked
ammunition, food, or manpower.
Sometimes they were worn out by
the constant attack, or by being cut
off from their supplies and **allies**.

Concentric castles

Castles with very strong defenses were very rarely attacked. Some of the strongest castles were built with **concentric walls**. This meant that the castle had two sets of walls, with the outer wall lower than the inner wall. Soldiers on the inner wall could fire over the heads of those on the outer wall. If attacking soldiers broke through the outer wall of the bailey, they were surrounded by archers. The inner wall was usually much stronger, with enormous gatehouses and towers.

The concentric castle was not a new idea. From the fifth century, the **Byzantines** in eastern Europe and the Middle East had built fortifications with concentric walls. When the **Crusader** knights fought in Palestine and Egypt, they saw castles without keeps, but with lines of very strong walls around their baileys instead. In their fight to make the Middle East

part of Europe, the Crusaders built enormous concentric castles there. The ruin of Krak des Chevaliers, the most famous of the Crusader castles, still stands in Lebanon.

When the Crusaders returned to Europe, they brought the idea of concentric walls with them. They knew that these castles were able to withstand the surprise attack with a very small number of defenders. The Tower of London is a good example of a concentric castle. Many were built in Wales by King Edward I, including Harlech, Beaumaris, and Caerphilly.

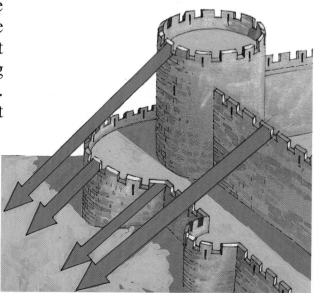

Right The concentric castle consisted of two sets of walls. The outer wall was lower than the inner wall, allowing defenders to fire over the heads of those below.

14

Above *The heavily fortified castle of Krak des Chevaliers showing its concentric defenses*

Left *The Tower of London. The central keep is surrounded by two sets of fortified curtain walls.*

Building a castle

The location chosen for a strong stone castle was of great importance. The location had to provide a natural defense, such as being situated on top of a high peak. It also had to be on an important route, near either a road or a river. The surrounding land had to be able to supply the castle with food and water. It was also useful if stone was plentiful in the area. Otherwise, heavy stones would have to be carried over long distances to the site on slow, crude carts.

A large stone castle could take many years to build. Large quantities of rubble were needed as the **hardcore** for the foundations of the walls and the buildings. Large quantities of stone from **quarries** and timber from forests were needed to build the castle.

The transport of these materials to the site and the construction of the castle had to be carefully planned. They both required a huge work force. The workers included masons, quarriers, smiths, and carpenters, as well as large numbers of unskilled laborers. The person in charge was often the master mason who supervised the work.

The stonemasons erected the shell of the building. They used cranes and hoists to lift the heavy materials to build the walls and towers. They often used a combination of rubble and stones mixed with mortar to hold the stone in place. A square style of

Left An early illustration of stonemasons building a castle tower. The stones are being hoisted by a pulley, while on the ground the stonemasons smooth the stones.

stone known as **ashlar** was often used for the outer surfaces of the castle and for strengthening the corners of the castle. The master mason would consult with the owner on materials.

Other workmen made the floors and doors of the castle. The last areas to be finished were the living quarters. The furniture was made by the carpenters. This included tables, benches, stools, chests, beds, and cupboards.

Above Castel Coco in Spain is a brick-built castle, an easier type to build than a stone castle.

In the fifteenth century, stone castles were replaced by castles built of bricks. While brick was unable to stand up to the force of the gunpowder now used in warfare, it made building quicker and cheaper, particularly in areas without building stone.

Castles as homes

A castle was a base from which soldiers could defend and control the surrounding countryside, town, or coastline for their **monarch**, or ruler. But a castle was also a home for many people—the family who owned the castle, their friends, relations, and servants.

Some castles were quite basic, with few comforts. Others were more grand, with attractive furniture and wall tapestries. The castle hall was a large room with long tables where the family could hold banquets when they were entertaining important visitors. The baron and his family and guests would sit together at a table toward one end of the great hall. Large numbers of cooks prepared the food in the kitchens. The kitchens were often separate from the living quarters because of the heat, smells, and danger of fire. Facilities in a castle were few—water could be collected from a well, but there were no bathrooms, even in the grandest castles.

Life in a castle was very public. Most people lived, ate, and slept crowded together. The castle owners had their own bedrooms, but most of the others slept crowded together in any space they could find—probably huddled near the fire rolled up in a blanket on the floor.

A castle was a busy, exciting place to live. There was always work to be done, and the castle was maintained by local craftsmen. Even small castles had carpenters, saddlers, blacksmiths, armorers, and shoesmiths. Larger castles would have cooks, candlemakers, launderers, and tailors. A castle could have hundreds of servants.

Life in a castle was not all hard work, and the people who lived there would find time to amuse themselves. They played games such as chess or checkers, or were entertained by the court jester or singing minstrels who traveled from castle to castle and brought news of distant happenings.

Right On a special occasion, the lord and lady of the castle would hold a banquet. While eating, they were often entertained by jugglers or minstrels.

Castles around the world

Above *The ruins of the Great Zimbabwe in southern Africa*

Below *The Red Fort at Delhi was built by the Moguls from Persia.*

There are castles in many parts of the world, built by both ancient and modern civilizations. About 1,500 years ago, the great walled city of Chichen-Itza in Mexico was built by the Mayan people. In southern Africa, there are still remnants of the Great Zimbabwe, built about 800 years ago by the Shona people.

In the Middle East, there are the remains of many of the Crusader castles. The construction of Krak des Chevaliers was started in the twelfth century and continued for over 150 years. Not only did this castle's steep position make it difficult to attack but the castle was also very heavily fortified with smooth concentric walls, which were impossible to climb. This made it difficult to capture the castle by storm. Krak des Chevaliers also had a vast storage space for food and a constant supply of fresh water so the defenders could not be forced out by starvation.

India has many beautiful castles, such as the Red Fort at Delhi, built during the Middle Ages by the Moguls from Persia. The Indian castles are surrounded by walls with powerful gates at the main entrances, which are often richly decorated. The gates were usually built to a great height to allow elephants and their riders to enter inside. The allies of the Moguls, the Rajputs, built the Amber Palace which overlooks the city of Jaipur.

Castles in Japan were built with the traditional Japanese design of smaller roofs standing on top of larger ones. Himeji Castle was built by a ruler in the fourteenth century and has since been reconstructed.

In the U.S.A., in the nineteenth century, log forts were built by the settlers as protection from North American Indians, who were angry at the invasion of their territory. One of these cavalry forts is Fort Laramie. Another famous fort is the Alamo, where Davy Crockett and Jim Bowie died in 1836.

In the U.S.S.R., the Moscow Kremlin is a castle with attractive domes on the roof. Until the seventeenth century, it was the home of the Russian czars (kings). The Kremlin is now the seat of the government of the Soviet Union.

Below In the U.S.A., log forts were built to protect traders and settlers from Native Americans. This is a painting of Fort William, one of the first log forts to be built.

Other famous castles

There are parts of the world that are very famous for their castles. The Loire Valley in France is well known for its châteaux. A *château* is a building such as a castle, a palace, or a country house. There are châteaux in France ranging from medieval fortresses to the later decorative palaces.

The château at Angers is a French medieval fortress designed to withstand sudden raids and long sieges. It has 17 towers and massive curtain walls. Some of the turrets have pointed roofs which were added to the castle later. Turrets are also a feature of German castles. Marksberg is the best preserved of the German castles built along the River Rhine. The castles were originally positioned so that troops inside them could attack boats who refused to pay a tax to the castle owner. Another famous castle is the Wartburg.

Right *This castle, called the Burg Pfalz, is built on a small island in the River Rhine in Germany.*

22

Spain is rich in castles, especially in the area that was called Castile. The Castel de Monte is a beautiful and famous Spanish castle with a **polygonal** plan. Outside it looks like a medieval castle, but the inside shows the influence of Arab culture with tapestries, beautiful rugs, and carpets. For the first time in a castle there was also the luxury of running water for baths. It was likely that this castle was used as a hunting lodge rather than as a fortress. The Castel Coco in Spain is a castle built of brick with decorations and massive turrets. But it also had strong corner walls and gun ports like a fortress. This castle was built to be attractive as well as heavily fortified.

Above The massive round towers of the medieval fortress at Angers in France

Left The Alcazar in Segovia, Spain, was built for a fifteenth-century king. From its high position, it defended the city walls.

Palaces

A palace is the official home of a ruler, such as a king, queen, prince, or emperor, or of an elected leader such as a president.

Many palaces were built when it was no longer necessary for rulers to live in castles for safety, but some were built much earlier. The Palace of Knossos on the island of Crete was built 4,000 years ago.

Château Azay-le-Rideau in France is a perfect example of a palace built in the style of a castle. The château has towers, turrets, and a moat. But there is nothing military about it—its features are for show. The purpose of the moat is to give a reflection of the château in its waters. There are wide staircases and big windows to let in the light.

Above *Château Azay-le-Rideau in France is a palace built in the style of a castle.*

Left *The famous Hall of Mirrors at Versailles in France has a mirrored wall that reflects sunlight from the opposite windows.*

Another fairy-tale palace is Neuschwanstein in Bavaria, begun by a Bavarian nobleman in the nineteenth century but never completed.

The Royal Pavilion is a splendid palace at Brighton in England. This was the seaside home of King George IV, built with oriental-style domes on the roof. The inside was decorated with Chinese furnishings.

The building of royal palaces was at its height in the eighteenth century. Palaces were the center of court life, full of courtiers and servants. King Louis XIV built a magnificent palace at Versailles, near Paris, to keep his nobles so busy with fashion that they would not attack him. Versailles was large enough to house all the nobles of his kingdom so he could keep them under his control.

With its gardens and parklands, Versailles was one of the most beautiful palaces in Europe and the standard by which others were judged.

Some palaces were built with a simpler design—for example, the Escorial near Madrid and the Winter Palace in Leningrad, Russia.

Some palaces are still used as homes for royalty or a ruler. Buckingham Palace is still the official home of England's Queen Elizabeth II. It contains rooms used for royal functions, the royal family's private quarters, and offices for their staff. The White House in Washington, D.C., serves as the official residence of the U.S. president. As the home of a ruler, it is a palace in all but name.

Left As the official home of the president of the U.S.A., the White House in Washington can be called a palace.

25

From manor houses to mansions

During the fourteenth century, large manor houses began to be built. These were fortified houses rather than large fortresses. Manor houses were usually purchased by wealthy merchants who felt the need to protect themselves, their families, and their possessions in unsettled times.

Most manor houses were built of stone and wood, but a few were built

of brick. Their roofs were tiled and their windows fitted with wooden shutters. Although manor houses had been built for hundreds of years, it was only at the very end of the Middle Ages that the building of a single room or hall gave way to a house with several stories. Some of the other rooms which were added were a kitchen, a chapel, and bedrooms.

Barons preferred the comfort of their manor houses, which were smaller and easier to control than a large, drafty castle. But, like castles, manor houses were designed for protection. Many were built like small castles without the high walls. They were usually fortified with strong doors, thick walls, and sometimes a moat. Fortified manor houses were often given the name of castles, such as Stokesay Castle in Shropshire, and Leeds Castle in Kent, England. The stone walls of Penshurst Castle, also in England, had battlements like a medieval castle. Many large manor houses copied this style.

By the sixteenth century, the manor house became a mansion. Changing methods of warfare meant that battles took place in the field rather than around a castle. This meant that houses built like fortresses were no longer needed. The houses of this period had smaller, cosier rooms and very large windows to make the rooms lighter. Attractive building designs and beautiful furniture made these houses very pleasant places to live.

Left *Feasting inside the great hall at Stokesay Castle, a fortified manor house in Shropshire in Britain*

Right *The style of a manor house often included some features of a castle. This manor house in Kent, England, has battlements and a moat.*

Mansions

A mansion is a large, grand home built by wealthy people, using timber, brick, or stone. Mansions are beautiful buildings, designed by **architects** and built by craftsmen using the best materials.

Left San Simeon in northern California is a mansion built in the style of a castle.

Attention to symmetry is important in the building of great houses. Mansions in the U.S.A. are large, fine houses. They were often built with an attractive flight of stairs at the entrance, and pillars leading to the roof. The outside of the mansions in South Carolina had clapboard walls, window shutters, and a staircase leading to the entrance hall.

In the eighteenth century, many grand houses were built in Britain. These **Georgian** mansions were large country houses with magnificent rooms for entertaining guests, and large numbers of bedrooms. They also had a library, a picture gallery, and a wine cellar. All of the rooms would contain graceful furniture and a stove for warmth. The main buildings of the mansion were joined by long corridors to the wings of the

Right A colonial mansion in Charleston, South Carolina

house where the kitchen and other rooms were situated. Life in a mansion was very comfortable. Plenty of servants were around to manage the work in the house and gardens.

Several famous buildings that were built as castles became mansions. Some people were still building homes in the style of castles early in the twentieth century. Castle Drogo, a mansion in Devon, England, was only finished in 1930. A famous castle-style mansion in the U.S.A. is San Simeon in California, built in the 1920s by millionaire William Randolph Hearst. This structure was put together using parts of buildings from all over Europe.

Mansions have replaced the castles of earlier times as grand homes built to last.

Glossary

allies Friendly countries or states that join together for a common purpose

ammunition A supply of war materials, such as arrows, gunpowder, or bullets

architect A building designer

armory A place for storing weapons

ashlar Cut stone with a smooth, straight finish

bailey A courtyard with buildings, surrounded by a fence

baron A member of the nobility with a title granted by a king or ruler

battlements Walls of a building with openings through which defenders can fire guns or arrows

Byzantines A group of people whose empire, also known as the Eastern Roman Empire, began as a part of the Roman Empire, but later took on its own identity.

civilizations Groups of people with highly developed cultures

civilians People not in the armed forces

concentric walls Two walls, one enclosed inside another

Crusaders Christians who wanted to take the Middle East from the Muslims in the Middle Ages

curtain wall A strong wall surrounding a bailey

drawbridge A bridge over a moat or ditch that can be drawn up

fortification A structure that protects and defends

gatehouse The fortified gateway to a castle from which the drawbridge and portcullis are raised

Georgian Something built or designed during the time between the reign of England's Kings George I and George VI (1714-1830)

hard-core Stones or rubble used as a foundation for buildings

keep The strongest part of a castle, usually a tower

monarch A ruler with a title like "king" or "emperor"

motte A large mound of earth on which a tower was built

murder-holes Holes in the roof of a passage through which defenders could drop objects on attackers

Normans Warriors from northwest France who took over England in 1066, led by William the Conqueror

palisade A strong wooden fence

portcullis A metal-covered gate that could be lowered quickly to block an entrance

privy A small bathroom

polygonal Many-sided

quarry A place where stone is dug from the ground

regimental standard The special emblem or flag for a particular group of soldiers

shell keep A wall around the top of a motte

siege A prolonged attack in which the attackers try to starve out or weaken the defenders

solar The private sitting room and sleeping chamber of a monarch

turrets Small towers on a building

wattle and daub Mud or clay plastered on to a framework of woven sticks

Books to read

The Middle Ages by Trevor Cairns (Lerner Publications, 1975)
The Castle Story by Sheila Sancha (Thomas Y. Crowell, 1979)
British Castles by R.J. Unstead (Thomas Y. Crowell, 1970)
Castles by Jenny Vaughan (Franklin Watts,1984)
The Castle Book by Michael Berenstain (David McKay Co., Inc., 1977)

Houses and Homes

Building Homes
Castles and Mansions
Homes in Cold Places
Homes in Hot Places

Homes in Space
Homes in the Future
Homes on Water
Mobile Homes

Picture Ackowledgements

The authors and publishers would like to thank the following for allowing their illustrations to be reproduced in this book: Aerofilms, p. 9; Mark Bergen, p. 19; Sally and Richard Greenhill, p. 5 (top); Michael Holford, p. 7; the Hutchison Library, pp. 12, 15 (both), 20 (top); John James, pp. 6, 8, 11, 13, 14, 24, 26; Leeds Castle Foundation, **cover**; National Trust Photographic Library, p. 27; Peter Newark's Western Americana, p. 21; Ronald Sheridan's Ancient Art and Architecture Collection, pp. 17, 20 (bottom), 22, 24 (top), 29; Topham, p. 10, 24 (bottom); ZEFA Picture Library, pp. 23 (both), 25, 28. All other pictures from the Wayland Picture Library.

Index